CONTENTS

Copyright © 1993 CPAS
First edition 1993. All rights reserved

Published by **CPAS**, Athena Drive, Tachbrook Park, WARWICK CV34 6NG.

ISBN 0 9077 5044 3
British Library Cataloguing-in-Publication Data.
A catalogue record for this book is available from the British Library

Cover design by Phil Gill• Text by Catherine Jackson
Printed by Unigraph Printing Services

Church Pastoral Aid Society • Registered Charity No 1007820
A company limited by guarantee

ABOUT THE AUTHORS

Mrs Eileen Moore has worked alongside her husband John in parish ministry in London, Coventry and Bournemouth. She is now working part-time at CPAS headquarters in Warwick. She has wide experience as a speaker and counsellor.

Mrs Shirley Broadhurst manages a book shop in Clitheroe, Lancashire and has been involved in leading training events and speaking at conferences for many years. She and her husband Ken were in parish ministry in the Midlands and the North of England.

The Rev Anne Hibbert is on the staff of CPAS as the Evangelism Co-ordinator and Adviser. She has worked in parishes in London and Leicester. She is the author of *Creating a Church for the Unchurched*, a CPAS Evangelism workbook.

Miss Isabel Anderson is a retired teacher and a reader at St Mark's Church, Leamington Spa. She is involved at Harnhill Manor, a Christian healing centre near Cirencester.

Mrs Susan Mileham is married to Paul and they have two children. She is a Museum Education Officer and an active member of St Mark's Church, Leamington Spa, where she is a Council and Diocesan Synod member.

The Rev Doreen Begernie was on the staff of CPAS for eleven years, including seven years as the head of Ministry Among Women. She is now retired and lives in Folkestone where she is actively involved in the ministry of St John's Church.

2

Learning to Listen © CPAS 1993

There are many books on the subject of listening, so what are we offering in this publication?

It is essentially a workbook to help many people, among them thousands of women leading groups in local churches, to explore listening in church, community and family. In working through these pages they will gain confidence to pick up the opportunities which are there in the every day happenings of life.

Norman Wakefield wrote in the *Counsellor's Journal* in 1981, 'Listening says "I want to understand you. I want to know you." It is one of the most basic ways to convey a sense of respect, to treat another person with dignity. Through this act we affirm in another person that God is willing to listen, that he eagerly waits for his troubled child to come to him and discover the compassion and deep concern of his loving Father. It makes available to the Holy Spirit a channel through which to communicate love and a helpful, appropriate response.'

Each chapter of this workbook has *Thinking Through* sheets with material for teaching a group. These may be photocopied, but essentially they are for a leader to help her to present the subject. These are followed by *Group Focus* sheets. Here you will find a number of exercises to help the group work at the topic. The number you use will depend upon the time available, but it is not intended that you use all of them in one session. You could use one as a follow-up exercise or even as an ice-breaker. Not all lead into group discussion or require talk-back, but all are thought provoking and have an ongoing usefulness as the group continues to explore the subject of listening. The third section, *Talking Points*, are sheets intended for photocopying and distribution to each member of the group to be used for discussion or as follow-up.

◆ *Listening to God* and *Listening to myself* will help groups to grow in Christ's likeness.

◆ *Listening to friends* and *Listening to neighbours* will encourage groups to share their faith.

◆ *Listening to young people* and *Listening to group members* will enable groups to understand and accept others.

Someone has said, 'God made us in the correct proportion: two ears but only one mouth.' This workbook is intended to help the average Christian to have the confidence to develop 'the gift of ears' (to quote the Primus of the Scottish Episcopal Church in 1985).

Can we afford not to develop this vital ministry in church, community and family?

'Take note of this, everyone should be quick to listen, slow to speak and slow to become angry.'

James 1:19

Listening to God

Some years ago, my daily habit as a rector's wife was to pray with the clergy team and their wives in church. A short liturgy was followed by a psalm, Bible reading and set and extempore prayers. We prayed for the day's activities, the church, the world and each other. It was a good start to the day. It was a rich part of it. We became close and committed. All our work was undergirded with prayer.

Waiting upon God

Life was full. Prayer times were full of words. And so I also began to include extra time, at home. I called it 'waiting upon God'. I needed some space and silence.

It was incredibly hard! The loud roar and clamour was amazing. I had expected stillness and peace! Distractions and words filled my mind. Would God ever come? I persevered yet it seemed God didn't speak during those quiet times so much as during the day. I fancied I heard his promptings, but so small was his nudge I could have missed it. Often, only in hindsight, I realized it was his voice, asking me to visit, to say something to someone, to listen to someone's heartache. But when I followed the nudges, and prayed with the despairing person God was directing me to, I saw specific and quick answers to prayer. When I talked to the person as prompted my words had a surprising impact. I paid more attention to these 'nudges'. I didn't want to fail to act, if it was God's voice prompting me.

Don't be foolish

We would be fools not to listen to God. After all, he created us, he knows us through and through. He has a purpose for our lives, which he longs for us to discover and fulfil. But he will never force us. We have the choice. He has provided the Bible, a manual, by which we can find out about himself, his teaching, ourselves and all the laws and principles of life. He wants us to listen.

If we don't listen to God we would be missing out on the best possible way of life. It would be like taking a mere mouthful at a grand banquet when there was a great feast for us freely to enjoy! We owe it to ourselves, to him and everyone else, to listen to this great God. He loves us. He has words of life—in abundance.

Who speaks?

Listening to God needs to be tinged with caution. I am wary of people who say, 'God told me to....' We cannot be one hundred per cent sure of pictures we see or prophecies we hear. God's confirmation is needed. Every voice is not necessarily God's. Often it is our own thoughts or ideas, even wishful thinking or imagination. It may be God. It could well be the evil one.

The supreme test is scripture. God does not contradict what is in his word, the Bible. Having spoken once, he does not contradict himself.

Another test is getting to know, as best we can, the mind of God, his personality and will. We need to be familiar, through scripture, with the kinds of pronouncements God makes on certain subjects. Just as the sheep discern the shepherd's voice, so we can become acquainted with what is in God's heart. We need to spend time in his presence as well as in his word, if we are to know his ways better.

The voice of our doubts, fears, pride or wishful thinking is often mistaken by us as God's voice. If we stand looking out of a window as dusk falls, our ability to see becomes poorer and poorer. We turn on the light inside the room. But what we now see, superimposed on our view outside, is a reflection of ourselves. So it is with listening to God. Our own needs and emotions sometimes reflect back in what we take to be a true picture of God. Only as we dim the light on our own lives, can we begin to see clearly.

One way to test, for instance, if we think God has spoken to us, is to ask him to confirm it through other people who don't necessarily know anything of the situation. The evil one is active in trying to counterfeit God's work and actions in order to deceive us and keep us from truth. True words of God have an authentic tone and ring clear and true. False words are tainted with fear, hurt or anxiety. They tend to fall flat. They lack the authority of God. Jesus' followers frequently recognized the authority of God in his words.

Learning to listen

How do I begin to set in motion a regular listening time? Take two sheets of paper. On the first write, 'what do I need?' and on the second, 'what's practical?' Without distinguishing between good and bad ideas, between the possible and impossible, jot down all you think you will need on the first sheet. Think of:

◆ time — how much, how often, how long?

◆ place — where would be the most suitable?
◆ comfort — furniture, posture, quietness.

Now, on your second sheet, translate these needs into something that's practical given your limited time and resources.

How do I get rid of distractions?

Distractions are inevitable; your thoughts will wander. But what can you do to help you focus?

How about:
◆ some deep, slow breathing in order to relax?
◆ using paper and pencil to jot down the many things you remember you mustn't forget?
◆ focusing on an object such as a tree, a flower or a lighted candle?
◆ watching the clouds and sky and the different colours of nature?
◆ listening to some music (hymns and songs) or to bird song?

Learning from others

I have learnt from others more experienced than I. I benefited from Joyce Huggett's *Listening to God*, Thomas à Kempis's *The Imitation of Christ* and Catherine Marshall's *Something More*. Brother Lawrence's *The Practice of the Presence of God* and Bunyan's *Pilgrim's Progress* are also valuable.

I have tried to take Jesus as the best model of all to follow. How did he relate to his heavenly father? Consider his

life. He was an obedient listener to God. He lived by the scriptures. For him the Old Testament taught and expressed God's mind, heart and will. Whether being tempted (Luke 4:4,8), challenged or when teaching his disciples and the people, 'it is written' was his oft-used phrase and conclusion for his arguments!

'God is most real when he ceases to be an object of enquiry and becomes someone who beckons.'

Alan Glendining

Our relationship with God

Relationships are the same whether they are with God, a friend or one of the family. The same parts of us, those that relate to other human beings, are those same parts we use to relate to God: our minds, feelings and spirits.

Four ingredients are needed in any relationship. Being aware of what they are helps us to check the quality of our relationships.

♦ Unconditional love
♦ Implicit trust
♦ Honour
♦ Understanding

So it is with God and us. There is a giving and receiving of love, trust, honour and understanding.

Understanding for us is very hard because God's ways are so different from our ways. He is perfect and all-knowing. We, in contrast, are by nature imperfect and selfish. Nevertheless, through two-way communication, it is possible to develop a deeper understanding. It is essential to spend time together and to listen and hear correctly what is being conveyed to us. The shepherd stories in both Old and New Testaments give lovely illustrations of the bonds which develop between the shepherd and his sheep. God is the shepherd and we his sheep. These stories not only speak of love and commitment, but show how God makes the first move in the relationship. 'The shepherd calls his own sheep by name and leads them out. When he has brought out his own, he goes ahead of them and his sheep follow him because they know his voice. But they will never follow a stranger because they do not recognize a stranger's voice.' John 10:3-5.

I am strangely moved when I read the shepherd accounts in the Bible and when I hear Christians tell of how they heard and eagerly responded to Jesus' call. My tears are a mixture of identifying with their joy and their discovery of God and a recognition of God's varied and apt method of calling, so suited to each individual. Chiefly, I suspect, my feelings are to do with Jesus' death on the cross, central to their understanding and mine as we made our first commitment to him. God communicates to his people in such a way that they simply have to respond. When they do so positively, it is wonderful.

Our chief aid

Undoubtedly, the Bible is our chief aid in listening to God. The most penetrating word we shall ever hear is in God's written Word.

♦ All foundations and teachings of our Christian faith are included in both the written Word and the living Word (Jesus Christ).
♦ The Bible contains the measure by which we can test everything — teaching about God and mankind and how we are to behave.
♦ The Bible has power to influence our minds, emotions and spirits — the living Word of the living God.

A final word. God is far more ready to hear us than we are to pray. Earnest prayer from his children is readily heard and understood. There are so many ways he comes to us. We need to thank him for what he is doing already in us and ask him for the best way forward.

GROUP IDEAS

Awareness walk

For 5 minutes or so encourage each member to go for a walk, alone, preferably outside. Ask them to note what they see, hear and smell. Ask God to speak to them as they walk. Share together the thoughts and feelings when the group re-assembles.

GROUP IDEAS

Names of God

There are many names of God in the Bible, in both Old and New Testaments. Encourage the group to recall some of these and to say them out loud for the benefit of the whole group. Allow a little time to meditate upon them and for God to speak. Conclude with worship, prayer and sharing together.

GROUP IDEAS

Where God speaks

In groups look at some Bible references on where God spoke to people: Exodus 19:3, Jeremiah 18:1, 1 Kings 19:9, Acts 9:6, Matthew 17:5, Revelation 1:19.

Make a list of where God spoke. When this is completed, encourage the group to share an occasion when God spoke to them. Spend time thanking God and praying that everyone will be ready to hear God speak anywhere.

GROUP IDEAS

How God speaks

Write up the Bible references below on an OHP. Ask the group, divided into pairs or small groups, to say how God spoke in Bible times. (If time is short use only two or three references.) After a few moments, list the findings against the relevant references for all to see. Allow the groups to list the different ways each has expressed. Share the difficulties of hearing God's voice.

Luke 1, Matthew 1:18-24 and 2:13-23, Acts 2, Acts 10, Acts 17, 1 Corinthians 14:27-33, John 2, John 4, Hebrews 1:1, Psalm 19:1-4, Acts 16, Luke 3:33, Luke 9:35.

GROUP IDEAS

Spirituality

In small groups write dictionary definitions of 'spirituality'. Share the definitions and decide, together, on the best. Would the group offer this definition to an enquiring young Christian, or would they change the words?

GROUP IDEAS

Fight the good fight

The apostle Paul uses pictures such as a race or a battle to describe Christian discipleship. What Bible pictures can the group remember? What other pictures are appropriate (e.g. a journey, growing up)? Which pictures mean most today?

Jesus at Martha and Mary's home

YOUR COMMENTS

- Read the story of Jesus staying with Mary and Martha from Luke 10:38-41. Read the text a second time: read it slowly, phrase by phrase, and imagine the scene in your mind's eye. (You may also like to read John 11:1-45 which tells you where the home was and more about the family.)

- Describe in your own words the scene before you.

- Consider the three characters: Mary, Martha and Jesus.
  1. What was each doing?
  2. What does Martha's appeal to Jesus say about her personality and her priorities?
  3. Why does Jesus commend Mary's attitude, when apparently she was leaving all the serving to Martha?
  4. What lessons can we learn from Jesus?

Consider

- Jesus is a guest in the home. More importantly, he is 'the Lord', teaching the family. He may even be preparing them for what they were to experience later. This same family will dramatically see the power of his words, 'I am the resurrection and the life' (John 11:25), when he brings back to life their dead brother, Lazarus.

- Jesus is probably having a meal, perhaps reclining on his side at the table. Mary, away from the table, is sitting at his feet. Jesus was the rabbi, instructing his pupil, a woman—an unheard of thing in those days! She was eager to learn.

- Jesus rebukes Martha for diverting Mary to less essential tasks. Mary chose the 'best dish' at the meal because she preferred listening to the teaching of the Kingdom. Martha's concern was to be a proper hostess, while Mary wanted to be a proper disciple. Jesus' concern was to serve and to fulfil his mission, not to have his rights as a guest.

Learning to Listen © CPAS 1993

God speaks today

The Bible is a record of God speaking to Moses, Abraham, the disciples and others. But God continues to disclose himself—today. His ways now are as many and varied as then.

◆ Eight-year-old Kate sensed God's presence. At bedtimes she said the prayer Mummy had taught her. She called God 'Heavenly Father'. Sometimes, if she couldn't sleep, she imagined the sky and pictures of wonderful landscapes. She sang all the choruses and hymns she could remember. It was as if she had discovered and entered God's 'home'. Although God seemed vast and far away, he could have been there in her room.

◆ Seventeen-year-old Margaret knew and loved God and loved Jesus. Suddenly she saw it all so clearly. As she listened to the minister, it seemed as if a light had been switched on in her head. Not only had Jesus died, he had died for her! And the same Jesus was alive now! She wanted to commit her life to him.

◆ A contemplative monk was asked, 'How do you spend all that time in prayer?' 'Well,' he replied, 'First, it's me and him. Then it's him and me. Finally, it's just him.'

◆ Elaine was praying about the new job her husband had been offered and in particular about the children. 'What about you, Elaine, are you willing to move?' The voice seemed audible, even above the noise of the vacuum cleaner she was using. She looked round expecting to see someone sitting in the room. Even before she fully realized that she was quite alone, she sensed it was God's voice. 'Yes, I'm willing to go, Lord!'

How does God speak today? Write down where and by what means.

God spoke to each of these people. Which accounts reflect your own experiences? Think of an occasion in your life when you believe God spoke to you.

YOUR COMMENTS

Listening to Neighbours

One of Jesus' best-known stories is of the Samaritan who helps a man who was mugged. The phrase 'good Samaritan' has passed into the English language, and the definition of a neighbour as 'anyone in need' has—we hope—passed into our hearts and lives.

A key point of the parable is that we don't always have a choice about who our neighbours are. They are made up of all kinds of people. And some will be easier to relate to than others. As people come into our lives they are influenced by us and change is brought about as we interact upon one another. Looking at our Bible reading in its simplest sense, neither the traveller nor the Samaritan were the same after their encounter.

If we belong to Christ, every contact we make is a golden opportunity to show something of the nature of God. He touches others through us, not only by what we say but by how we act.

One of the greatest problems of the 1990s is that most people do not have a sense of need. Today there wouldn't have been any need for the Good

Samaritan to have become involved with the traveller. He could have simply phoned for the ambulance! Needs are there, however, but they are more often emotional rather than physical. This makes them harder to recognize. And our 'neighbours' are more difficult to get alongside.

Listening is the key

Solomon asked God for a listening heart—see 2 Chronicles 1:10. 'Give me wisdom and knowledge,' he said, 'that I may lead this people, for who is able to govern this great people of yours?'

Most translations use the word 'understanding' or 'discerning', but the Hebrew word literally means 'hearing'. Solomon knew that to be an effective leader he had to be a good listener. This highlights how crucially important listening is in forming relationships and developing insight.

God listens

God listens. For example, God listened when Abraham sent Hagar and Ishmael away. They became exhausted; the mother wept in despair. But she is told by the angel that 'God had heard the boy crying' (Genesis

21:8-21). Indeed the name Ishmael means 'God hears'.

The Psalmist repeatedly acknowledged that the Lord heard him as he cried out. 'Away from me, all you who do evil, for the Lord has heard my weeping. The Lord has heard my cry for mercy; the Lord accepts my prayer.' (Psalm 6:8-9)

As he stood in front of Lazarus' tomb, Jesus knew that God was listening to him. 'Father', he said, 'I thank you that you have heard me. I knew that you always hear me, but I said this for the benefit of the people standing here, that they may believe that you sent me.' (John 11:41-42)

The fact that God listens tells us that he recognizes mankind's basic need for a listener.

Be relaxed

Listening skills can be developed. There are a few who find listening is a natural gift but although a lot of people say 'I'm a good listener', it is only rarely true.

In helping others there is always a sense of inadequacy. Often we feel that because someone has confided in us

they expect us to have the answer to their problem. This fills us with apprehension and stops us listening properly. It is important to be relaxed in order to listen. Look at 1 Peter 3:8 where we are told to be 'sympathetic, love as brothers, be compassionate and humble'.

Don't be afraid

Don't be afraid of silence. Be at peace in it and keep giving the situation to God. Jesus is the burden bearer: no matter how heavy the burden is, it is Jesus not you who can lift it.

Don't be afraid of emotions. Anxiety and rage are often the result of 'fear', and fear is a knowledge of the lack of resources. To be allowed into a person's real feelings means that you are nearly at the point of total honesty.

Don't be afraid for you have nothing to lose. People everywhere are looking for a purpose and they are looking for answers—but mostly in the wrong places. Explain that

you don't claim to know everything or to have all the answers, but that you do know that it works for you! There is no more powerful argument than that.

People differ

In listening to others we will need to approach their needs through many different methods as both people and situations are different. There is no hard and fast rule.

Firstly, we must be prayerful in our approach.
Be positive in prayer.
Be purposeful in prayer.
Be particular in prayer.

Secondly, we must be simple in our approach. Simplicity confounds people.

Thirdly, we must be sensitive. After many hours of listening an opportunity may come for you to be bold, with the confidence which Christ gives.

Use the Bible as your authority but not out of context or as an excuse for no further

participation on your part. We have all been at the receiving end of the slick Bible quotes that leave us feeling more attacked and desolate than comforted.

Listening is a primary means of showing God's love. It also provides the foundation for wise counsel. I have often found that careful listening leads to the real source of the problem, which can be quite different to the perceived one.

Six key points

How can we listen to a neighbour? We may feel that our neighbour's problems require far more skill than we can offer. Sometimes they do, and good listeners are quick to recognize when they are getting our of their depth. But nine times out of ten we can be genuinely helpful by simply listening. We may not—and probably don't—have the answers. But we can listen. And through our listening God can bring healing. The Samaritan's two coins are our two ears!

> 'It is impossible to over emphasize the immense need human beings have to be listened to....
>
> In most conversations, although there is a good deal of talk, there is not real listening; such conversations are no more than a dialogue of the deaf.'
>
> **Paul Tournier**

As we listen we need to:

1 Show respect. Respect gives value to the person one is listening to. We must avoid being patronizing.

2 Be genuine or 'real'. There is no point in pretending to be something we are not.

3 Offer empathy. We need to feel with the person and put ourselves in their place. Their problems may then look very different.

4 Be positive. There is a need to avoid vagueness in our comments. We should avoid 'why' questions as they sound judgmental. It is better to use 'how?' For example, how does it make you feel?

5 Consider confrontation. Confrontation is rarely appropriate but can sometimes have a place in forming solutions.

6 Focus. We should be aware of what is going on *now* and *listen*.

Pressure points

Pressure originates with the activities of life. Change is the most common ingredient of pressure.

Childhood and youth

Right from our earliest days we face pressure. The pressure on our young people is enormous. Their peer group, who are equally insecure, inexperienced and often rebellious, have an enormous influence. Our children don't like to be different, and the power of the peer group becomes evident in their attire, speech and habits. These days there are other pressures: drugs, alcohol, sexual permissiveness. These all exercise powerful stresses on young people.

We live in a rebellious age; youngsters are indulged from the cradle and are given little of the security that discipline brings. They are unable to absorb the frustrations and pressures of life.

Anger and hostility impair good judgement and bad decisions only compound the pressure of life. Proverbs 22:15 says, 'Folly is bound up in the heart of a child, but the rod of discipline will drive it far from him.' Rebels are usually estranged from those who would counsel them the best, and so they turn back to

their peer group for guidance.

Strong young people are usually the product of a strong home. It takes time to communicate love and resourceful values. We need to see time spent with our children as a necessity. It needs to climb to the top of our priority list.

The teenage years

Pressures of teenage children are among the hardest to cope with. 'It was so much easier when they were young', we say! The demanding of adult privilege, without the taking of adult responsibility, is a dilemma which parents and teenage children constantly face. Teenagers test every rule. It will shatter their confidence if their parents become less than the stabilizing influence in their lives.

Character is never built by self indulgence—success is rooted in self discipline.

Marriage and parenthood

Marriage is a source of pressure. Sometimes there is a lack of money, with both partners having to work. Because of the glitz that surrounds sex, there is sexual pressure, with little time given to romance and caring.

Relationships become selfish and one or the other feels 'used'.

Parenthood creates pressure, particularly for the young mother. She may have to grapple with a fractious child. She may find herself without 'money of her own'. Within the church family we need to be aware of these pressures and be honest about them. We must learn to relax with our babies and enjoy them, thanking God continually for them.

Pressure on the single

Possibly the greatest pressure for single people is loneliness. One in five of the adult population live alone. A sense of inferiority can creep in, a feeling of being 'less than one was intended to be'. If this is allowed to get a hold, the person will be less than God intended! This is because thinking affects how we feel and feeling decides how we behave. The single person needs to be encouraged to be outward looking, to learn more about others.

Contentment can be learned.

Divorce

One in two marriages ends in a divorce. There are millions of divorcees who feel they are victims of failure and rejection.

They are left with a host of disintegrated dreams. This is a tremendous pressure and from it arises feelings of anger, guilt, embarrassment and shame.

Those who continue to care for children after their marriage has broken up have the added pressure of coping with their children's anger.

Retirement pressure

Retirement brings feelings of 'being on the scrap heap' and 'feeling redundant'. There is the pressure of having time— perhaps for the first time—and not knowing what to do with it. Financial insecurity and failing health loom large and make many fearful.

Change

Change is a natural part of life, yet it always produces pressure.

A person's perception of how much control they have over a situation determines how much pressure it causes them. Being 'in control' reduces pressure to bearable levels. We need to have hope. We can stand anything if we know it won't go on forever.

I always say, 'If it's a problem, it has a solution. If it hasn't a solution, it's a fact of life and must be lived through.'

Our attitudes are formed by what we think. What we think determines the way we feel, and the way we feel decides how we behave.

The most important ingredient in reducing pressure is mental attitude. It is very important to get our thinking right.

'The first duty of love is to listen.'

Paul Tillich

The example of Christ

In the life of Jesus all the emotions and feelings of an ordinary person can be seen. The Gospels record that Jesus was tired, hungry, sad. In Gethsemane he wept. On the cross he felt abandoned.

In the epistles, the compassion of Christ is urged upon believers.

Forgive one another: 'Forgiving each other, just as in Christ God forgave you.' (Ephesians 4:32)

Comfort one another: 'The Father of compassion and all comfort.' (2 Corinthians 1:3-4)

Love one another: 'Taught by God to love each other.' (1 Thessalonians 4:9)

Encourage one another: 'Encourage one another and build each other up.' (1 Thessalonians 5:11)

Accept one another: 'Accept one another, then, just as Christ accepted you.' (Romans 15:7)

GROUP IDEAS

Points to ponder

Divide those present into groups and ask each to take a different point to ponder. At the end, groups should come together to reflect on what they've decided. Was the emphasis on talking or listening?

♦ Someone is faced with major surgery. What do you say?

♦ A woman finds her husband is unfaithful and needs to talk. How do you handle this?

♦ Your neighbour is watching his wife die. What can you say?

♦ The couple across the road have a teenage son who has gone 'off the rails'. They are very bitter. How do you respond?

GROUP IDEAS

Hidden meaning

In small groups share what lies behind these statements and how they can be handled.

'I might have to go into hospital for a small operation, but I expect it's nothing really.'

'I wanted to talk to the vicar about this but he's busy and this is a trifle really.'

'This is the third time in a month that I've tried to stop smoking. I'm a useless Christian.'

'There's a lot of talking at work, about redundancies. But I don't think it will affect me.'

'Ever since my husband died last year, I can't seem to get myself going, but I guess I'm just lazy.'

GROUP IDEAS

Newsprint and prayer

Supply each small group of, say, four people, with a fairly recent newspaper. Use a local paper if possible. Ask them to use the newspaper to see the needs of neighbours. Supply a large sheet of paper (such as the reverse side of wallpaper), scissors, paper glue and felt-tip pens, and ask each group to make a montage from the newspaper which will be a focus for prayer for the coming week. Allow time to use this in prayer with the group.

Evaluate your listening skills

1. Other people think I am a good listener.

Usually/Sometimes/Never

2. If I don't agree with what is being said I tend to 'shut off'.

Usually/Sometimes/Never

3. I know how to 'prompt' in order to bring out more of a person's problems.

Usually/Sometimes/Never

4. I can listen to a person for:

5 Minutes/15 Minutes/30 Minutes

5. My mind wanders when I feel 'I have heard it all many times before'.

Usually/Sometimes/Never

6. I know when to 'shut off' and yet appear to be listening

Usually/Sometimes/Never

7. I interrupt others when they are speaking.

Usually/Sometimes/Never

8. I consider listening is a very important part of a relationship.

Usually/Sometimes/Never

◆ Can you see where your strengths and weaknesses lie?

◆ Ask a friend who is honest, fair and knows you fairly well, to answer the questions about you! Offer to do it for that friend.

◆ Share ways in which you can help each other to improve your listening skills.

YOUR COMMENTS

Listening to Friends

What immediately leaps to mind when the word 'evangelism' is used? Do we think of a nervous person standing on a doorstep with a huge, floppy Bible? And as we dwell on this picture do we silently pray, 'Please God don't ever let that person be me!?'

We may be all too familiar with Jesus' parting words to his disciples, 'Go and make disciples of all nations', yet we feel immobilized by them. We live with a sense of guilt that we are not doing our 'bit' for the Lord. Guilt, however, may be inappropriate. It may be founded on misconceptions. What is evangelism? And what is our Lord asking us to do?

Evangelism is not...

Evangelism is not about an occasional raid by a visiting evangelist celebrity. And after he or she has gone everyone breaths a sigh of relief and goes back to their normal church activities.

Evangelism is not a system or package which you have to learn and digest. Nor do you occasionally have to burst into action and assault someone with the 'four spiritual laws' or 'five things God really wants

you to know'.

Evangelism is not about standing on a street corner giving out pieces of paper about your church.

Evangelism is...

There may be an element of evangelism in all the above. But true evangelism is about one person telling another, in the most natural way possible, about the life, death and resurrection of Jesus and the relevance of this today. C H Spurgeon, the famous 19th century British preacher and evangelist, described sharing our faith as 'one beggar telling another beggar where to get bread'. Evangelism draws attention to the needs of the recipient and the generosity of the giver. God will not give us a stone when we want bread. It also speaks of equality because a Christian is not on higher ground than the person he or she is talking to. The ground is completely level around the cross of Christ. The only difference between the two hungry beggars is that one has been fed and knows where food is always available.

There is no great mystique about it. Evangelism is simply telling a fellow 'searcher'

where they can obtain food. It also reminds us that we cannot bring this good news to others unless we personally have come to 'taste and see that the Lord is good'. (Psalm 34:8)

Sharing our faith is not just a matter of proclaiming the good news of Christ and eliciting decisions for Christ by getting people to raise their hands or sign a commitment card. Our goal should be to fulfil the 'Great Commission' by making disciples of Jesus Christ. A disciple is a learner. And evangelism which is truly evangelism is not only about helping a person to make a decision for Christ but also about helping them to live their lives for him and serve him in their local church. One excellent definition of evangelism is: 'To evangelize is to present Jesus Christ in the power of the Holy Spirit, that all people shall come to put their trust in God through him, to accept him as their Saviour and serve him as their King in the fellowship of his church.'

Sharing our faith
Many Christians feel inadequate when they hear accomplished evangelists explain the Christian faith. They think, 'I just can't be like them.' That is

probably true. But it doesn't mean that we cannot speak about how God is at work in our lives. As David Watson once said, 'It is important to stress that not every Christian is called to be an evangelist. All are witnesses to Christ, and must be committed to the church's task of evangelism, but only some are evangelists.'

To some a special gift of evangelism is given. These evangelists are able to create opportunities for sharing and explaining the good news. Theirs is the role of standing at the front and addressing a crowd. Theirs is the faith (perhaps) which isn't plagued with doubts, and theirs is the knowledge to convince the sceptic.

But most of us are not evangelists. We are witnesses. We can only speak of what little we know of God's love. And we can only do it in our own, quiet way. Those of us who are witnesses usually befriend people and work in response to their questions.

Team work
Sharing our faith is about team work. Both witnesses and evangelists need to work hand in hand. For example, there may be an evangelistic supper party. The role of a witness means inviting friends—people who may be interested in the faith which the witness owns. Then, at the supper, the evangelist speaks about Jesus and hopefully brings some of these people to a point of commitment.

The evangelist may only be working in the church or community for a short time. It is up to the witnesses to introduce their friends to the local church and ensure there is appropriate follow-up to the questions asked or decisions made at the evangelistic supper party.

A role to play
The Bible Society's recent publication *Finding Faith Today—how does it happen?* states that most people become Christians gradually—and the process takes an average of four years. It also says that for most people their spouse or partner, Christian friends, ministers and children are far more likely to be factors leading to faith than evangelistic sermons or books. All of us, then, have a vital role to play in a friend or neighbour becoming a Christian.

'Listening is rubbing my spiritual finger along someone's soul and so feeling for the cracks.'

Trevor Partridge

Looking at the results, John Finney who supervised the research said this about people who had recently become committed Christians: 'For them the Christian faith is about relationships. Nearly all defined a Christian, not so much by what he or she believed, but in terms of friendship and the effect of faith upon their life.'

We all have a role to play because all of us can share our stories of how God is at work in our lives. So then, let's all pray for opportunities to share our faith, and when one arises, let us take a deep breath, be ourselves and talk naturally about the God we know.

That's what evangelism is all about.

'It is the province of knowledge to speak and it is the privilege of wisdom to listen.'

O W Holmes

Why suffering?

'Cursed is the ground because of you: through painful toil you will eat of it all the days of your life. It will produce thorns and thistles for you, and you will eat the plants of the field. By the sweat of your brow you will eat your food until you return to the ground, since from it you were taken; for dust you are and to dust you will return.'

Genesis 3:17-19

Often when we are witnessing about our faith, the question will arise, 'OK, if God is a God of love why is there so much suffering in the world?' The person may go on to describe some horrific news item which they have seen on the television recently. What is our reaction? Do we quickly try and move on to another subject? Or do we try to pick up the real agenda, the person's own suffering or sense of loss?

Hidden agendas

The question about world suffering often stems from a personal experience that an individual has never come to terms with. They may still be feeling deeply hurt and broken, and may even be holding God responsible. It is important to be sensitive at all times and to listen. It may not be appropriate on your first encounter to ask personal questions. However, as your friendship grows, you may be able to have a deeper conversation and discover that your friend's mother suffered with cancer for many years or a close relative died in a car accident.

Your friend may often ask 'Why me, why my family?' Don't rush in with short, trite answers. Don't throw back

Bible verses. Your role may just be to listen and to empathize. Your friend may become angry and tearful. You could be the first person they have spoken to about this personal tragedy in years; it may have been welling up inside them for a very long time.

Jesus our brother

If your friend is upset, you may not be able to say much about God at all at this point. Your role is to listen, to comfort and to remember what they are telling you. Later, when the person is calmer, talk about Jesus and how he had compassion on people in their sufferings. You may want to talk about Jesus' encounter with the woman at Nain and the compassion he felt for her (Luke 7:11-17). Or refer to his own tears shed outside the tomb of his best friend Lazarus (John 11:35).

At all times stress that Jesus was fully human. He knew what it was like to suffer. He felt pain, anguish and separation from God. Above all he experienced a vile, unjust death. There is no 'answer' to the question of suffering. But we do worship a God who has shared it alongside us.

Origins of suffering

We have to admit our ignorance. We do not have the full explanation for evil and suffering.

God created the universe perfect, but humanity through free will chose to disobey God—and evil consequences spread through the creation because of continued disobedience to God's will and purpose.

We must not overlook the presence of disobedience in each of us. If God executed judgment without mercy, no one would survive. Much of the suffering in the world is brought about through people being out of touch with God and his world, and thus being inhumane, selfish, greedy, unjust, spiritually blind and sometimes stupid.

The Bible clearly shows how Jesus accepted suffering as an inescapable ingredient of life. But he made it clear that we must never assume personal disaster is God's direct judgment for personal sin (Luke 13:1-5). Many who suffer look for a reason. God, they say, must be punishing them; there must be a purpose behind their predicament.

Jesus rejected this sort of thinking. Suffering may be the consequence of mankind's wilful rebellion against God, but Susan's cancer is not God's retribution because she hates her mother in law!

Remember these points which we may be able to use in our conversations.

♦ Suffering was not God's original intention for his world.
♦ Sometimes there is an element of human responsibility.
♦ Jesus was dedicated to the relief of suffering.
♦ Jesus taught that there was something worse than physical suffering.
♦ Jesus himself experienced suffering that was totally undeserved.
♦ There will one day be an end to suffering.

Bishop Michael Marshall has said: 'Only Christianity, of all world religions, has a problem about suffering, because it insists that God cares. In Islam, fatalism takes over and speaks of all suffering as "the will of Allah"—Allah who displays power more than love. In Buddhism, there is an unwillingness to be realistic about suffering. "In the midst of sorrow there is no Nirvana, and in Nirvana there is no sorrow."'

It is important to stress that Jesus shared our suffering at the deepest possible level, and cared for those caught in suffering. Jesus was no mere spectator to the anguish of the world, and indeed showed through the miracles that God has effective power over evil and its results.

'Give every man thine ear, but few thy voice.'

William Shakespeare, Hamlet

Effective listening

♦ Try to suspend initial judgement—listen in a non-evaluative way and only evaluate when you have fully understood.

♦ Know yourself and your own areas of sensitivity and doubts.

♦ Always seek clarification where necessary and help the person to help you understand what their situation is. Don't be afraid to repeat back what you think you have heard them say. If necessary ask for correction.

♦ Give yourself *time* to listen. Be prepared to respond, but not too quickly.

♦ Eliminate distractions as far as possible, e.g. turn the television or radio off! But remember that many young people can listen in a noisy environment.

♦ Be alert to emotional undercurrents that may be beneath what is being said. Watch for non-verbal clues, for example avoiding eye contact.

GROUP IDEAS

Research and share

Put people into small groups with paper and felt-tip pens. Ask them to write down a list of what prevents Christians from sharing Jesus with their friends. Allow 8 minutes and then discuss.

GROUP IDEAS

Can you hear me?

Divide into pairs. Ask one person to take the role of an enquirer. Give her a character to play such as a single parent who has questions about the kind of world her child will be growing up in. The enquirer asks, 'Why is there so much evil around? Isn't God supposed to be a God of love?' Allow the two to talk for 5-10 minutes. At the end the enquirer should report on how well the other listened. Then swap roles.

GROUP IDEAS

Brainstorm

Ask the group to suggest what others fear about becoming a Christian. Allow 8 minutes. List suggestions on OHP or large sheet of paper without comment or discussion. Accept even the most obscure ideas.

(The value of this kind of exercise is that people become more open about their own fears and misgivings.)

GROUP IDEAS

Journeys

In groups of 3 or 4, write a letter to a visiting preacher, giving careful directions on how to find your church. Allow 5 minutes and then read out some of the letters. Summarize together what is necessary for good directions (e.g. listing landmarks, signposts and obstacles). Encourage the group to share the landmarks, signposts and obstacles for guiding someone on a Christian journey of faith for the first time.

GROUP IDEAS

A good thing

Put the group into pairs to talk to one another in turns for 2 minutes each. Each person should talk, uninterrupted, about something for which she has a great deal of enthusiasm, For example, it might be her family or a new hobby. Then ask them to repeat the exercise, but this time to talk about Jesus, their faith, and why they go to church.

GROUP IDEAS

Prayer

In twos or threes talk about the friends people are in contact with who are not yet Christians. Pray for them and for opportunities to share the Christian faith and express Christian support and love.

Learning to Listen © CPAS 1993

Telling our story of faith

For many of us sharing our faith is one of the hardest things to do for God.

- Often as Christians we feel inadequate. There is fear that we will not be able to express our faith and we may end up saying:
  'I am just not that kind of person.'
- Some *have* spoken, but got into difficulties:
  'I have tried it before but it's just too embarrassing.'
  'I became tongue-tied.'
- Others of us feel we haven't got enough knowledge of the gospel and therefore could be caught out by difficult questions.
  'I won't know what to say.'
- Some of us may have experienced aggressive evangelism which has put us off totally.
  'I felt I was being threatened and I would never do the same to someone else.'
- For some of us our Christianity is personal.
  'My faith is private. I like to keep it that way. It's not proper to talk openly about religion.'

Are any of these reasons true for you? Are there any other reasons?

What would help you overcome this reticence to share your faith?
- Attending a practical course on how to share your faith?
- Practising on a Christian friend!?
- Accompanying someone on an evangelistic visit who is used to sharing their faith?
- Something else?

Clues from Acts
Read Acts 1:8, 2:38-47 and 4:18-37. The Acts of the Apostles offers some clues on how the first Christians shared their faith.

- What clues are there in each passage for how the early church grew?
- What gave the first Christians the incentive and the enthusiasm to share their faith?
- What seemed to be their priorities?

YOUR COMMENTS

Listening to Myself

What am I like—really like? Every morning, when I do my hair, I see my reflection in a mirror. So I have some idea what I look like. Three years ago, after an abdominal operation, the surgeon said he'd 'had a good look round—nothing else to worry about', so someone knows part of what I look like inside. But that's only my body. What am I really like?—personality, character, skills, hobbies? What do I like doing, and what avoid? Who am I? Can I really understand myself—my joys, hopes, fears? Can I control my thoughts or be responsible for my hidden motives?

The second commandment

You may be thinking 'I'm not sure I want to get to know myself. Am I worth listening to? I don't like myself very much. Dare I try to discover the real me?'

Jesus told us (Mark 12:28-34) that the first commandment is to love God with every part of our being. The second is to love others in the same way as we love ourselves. It seems we can't love our neighbour unless we love ourselves too. We need to love ourselves if we are going to love others.

Love leads to loving

I'm not talking about becoming enamoured with our own reflections like Narcissus in the Greek legend. No, I mean coming to a godly appreciation of ourselves.

Paul wrote to the Roman church, 'Think of yourself with sober judgment.' (Romans 12:3) This sounds very serious and hard but it isn't—if we start in the right place, with God. God says in many verses of the Bible (for example, Isaiah 43:4, John 3:16, Ephesians 2:4 and 1 John 4:10) that he loves us more than we will ever fully realize. He has demonstrated it in sending Jesus, his son, to be our saviour and risen Lord. He made us because he wanted us in his world. He has watched over us because he wants us here, now. We are unique and loved unconditionally by the living God.

As our Father in heaven loves us so much, should we not also accept ourselves, appreciate ourselves, care for ourselves, love ourselves?

A lost cause?

When we were lost and helpless, God reached down to us in love. He has paid the price of our salvation, in Jesus on the cross. Now Jesus has been raised to life again and enthroned in heaven; God has given us his Holy Spirit, his life in us. We have confidence for the future. Almighty God is totally committed to you and to me and to us together in his family, the church.

Facing the truth

The Holy Spirit is at work in us making us holy. Of course, we may not like ourselves. But change is in the air. Growth and development are on the programme. Maturity and wholeness are the target. God loves us too much to leave us as we are.

I well remember a time when I was battling with a nasty bit of me. I had said, 'I'm sorry Lord, this is awful' several times. Eventually, I was worn out with the struggle. I leaned back in my chair and in my heart said, 'Yes, Lord, I agree with you. This (naming it) is really me.' His response came to me so clearly, 'Oh Isabel, I love you so much. I've known all along. I'm so glad you admit it. Now I can start the healing and the transformation.' In such ways does our gracious God

invite our co-operation in becoming the people he would have us to be.

God's unconditional love, coupled with his perfect knowledge of our sinful depths, brings relief and reassurance when our hearts condemn us.

King David knew that God desires truth in our inner being (Psalm 51:6) and tells us that he prayed that his thinking would please God (Psalm 19:14). Yet Jeremiah says that our hearts are deceitful (Jeremiah 17:9). So, how do you and I know that if we listen to ourselves we will not be led astray by lies and distortions?

Many voices from society as well as echoes from the past clamour for our attention. How can we distinguish to whom we are listening? I'm comforted by the fact that Jesus said his sheep would hear his voice and be able to follow. Listening directed by the Holy Spirit who leads into truth will be godly even if sin is exposed or pain revealed as part of the process.

Recognizing our emotions

One way I listen to myself is to check how I am feeling. The purpose is not introspection. (Why I am feeling as I am and what I need to do about it, if anything, may take some time. To keep a finger on the pulse of my emotions only takes a moment.)

My routine goes like this: How am I feeling just now? Relaxed,

perhaps, or edgy, irritable, peaceful, anxious, sad, curious, impatient or one of a hundred other possibilities? Often I can trace the reason for the feeling. If I can, that's OK. But if I can't, I may need to hold my emotions in check because I have more immediate responsibilities. For example, if I feel angry or fearful, and my friends will be in for tea in a moment, I need to do something with myself quickly. God can (and does when I ask him) hold my anger or fear for me, so I don't damage others. Later I find an opportunity with more time in which to sort it out properly.

The work of the Spirit

When we don't recognize our feelings, they tend to control us and get out of hand. Jesus was fully human and experienced a wide range of emotions. Always completely in control, he expressed his compassion, joy, anger and sorrow appropriately and without sin.

Since I've listened to myself and become aware of my emotions, I have expressed them firstly to God in prayer. The Holy Spirit has begun to show me how to handle them in a more godly way than before.

When I've admitted I'm anxious, feeling down or lonely, God has made his presence very real and allayed my fears. Also he has pointed out little bonuses of joy throughout the day—children playing, the colours of a nearby garden or a reminder of his promises. So my serenity has

increased and brought frequent thanksgiving.

Admitting to God what our inner voice is saying opens us to the ministry of the Spirit of God at a deep level. We're listening to ourselves and letting God meet us where we are. The result is that we become more sensitive to others, to how they are feeling and what they need. So Christ in us touches them for their healing, release and maturity.

'I must cultivate awareness and first of all awareness of myself. I must know myself before I can know God or anyone else. It is hardly possible for us to be too silent while we listen. If I can't stay with the pain of what is being shared it will be because it reminds me of undealt-with pains of my own.' Peter Graham

---

It's being loved and accepted in Jesus, by God the Father, that is the start of it all.

GROUP IDEAS

Those were the days

In small groups agree a time of life and place such as 'aged 4-6 years, at home, at the weekend'. Together keep silence for a few moments and remember. After a minute or two ask people to share the echoes of their past: voices such as 'eat up', 'shut the door', 'Come on, hurry up!'

Whose voices were loudest?

Take another few moments to remember school days, say 13-14 years old. Share together. Again, highlight those voices best remembered. Some of the messages were probably:

Instructions (e.g. Clean your teeth, Don't forget...)
Principles (e.g Never trust strangers, Money matters most, Save time..)
Judgements (e.g You're slow, You're not as good as... You must try harder...)

GROUP IDEAS

Alone in a crowd?

Ask people to remember their first visit to an unfamiliar church. Did they feel welcomed, helped to be at ease? Or were they alone in a crowd?

How do people who have come to your local church view the welcome they were given? If the group doesn't know the answer, could members find out by talking to some recent arrivals? Do so, and pool your findings for your group and perhaps your church council to discuss.

GROUP IDEAS

What I've always wanted to say

Write up on an OHP or large sheet of paper the following:

Likes and dislikes
Strengths and weaknesses
Fears and joys
Successes and failures

Put the group into pairs and ask them to share together about their own reactions to these topics. After about 10/15 minutes each person should seek permission of her partner to share one thing with the whole group.

GROUP IDEAS

Coping with loneliness

Use the chart on page 27. Photocopy it on to an OHP acetate or give out copies to each person in the group. Being on your own may be uncomfortable ('I'm lonely') or it may feel comfortable ('Marvellous—I've time for myself'). What are the emotions people experience? And what are the actions/reactions which follow? For example, a lonely person may seek company. In the boxes on the chart list some of these actions; link the boxes together with arrows if appropriate. Conclude with a practical statement of what a person can do.

Read Psalm 137 (a song of sorrow), Psalm 138 (a song of praise) and Psalm 139 (a song of acceptance).
What are our songs of sorrow, praise and acceptance?

GROUP IDEAS

Life as a tree

Think of a tree with roots, trunk, branches, leaves, berries, flowers and fruit. Think of it as tall, broken, dying, young or old. Think of it in all seasons, weathers and situations.

Ask each person to draw themselves as a tree with the roots, trunk and branches etc. What sort of tree do they picture themselves as? Encourage them to add anything they like to the tree to illustrate their life. They can add as much as they want to remember and include those things that they hope will happen.

In groups of 3 or 4, ask people to share their trees and to look up one of the Bible passages below. Allow time for sharing and prayer in each small group.

Psalm 1	(verse 3, in particular)
Psalm 128	(verse 3)
Jeremiah 17	(verses 5 - 8)
John 15	(verses 1 - 8)

GROUP IDEAS

'Honest to God' Psalms

Choose one of the following Psalms: 30, 32, 35, 37.

Eavesdrop on David talking to God and telling God how he felt. Identify negative and positive feelings. What emotions can the group discover? What do we fret over? Is there anything here about forgiveness? Is there anything we feel we could never ask God for? Ask the group if they think David would have been embarrassed to know that they were listening to his soul-thoughts.

GROUP IDEAS

Fine, thanks

In Sunday morning conversations, one of the most used replies to 'how are you?' is 'fine, thanks'. Often people are anything but!

What is the real truth underneath the mask of 'fine'? We get so used to expecting others not to listen to us, we don't know what we would say if we were asked.

Plan a group meeting with the title *Getting clear what I'd like to say to my local church*. Ask each member to spend a bit of time beforehand thinking with the Holy Spirit's help. When you come together, ask each one to list three aspects of church life that are of personal value to them. Pool your thinking to make a combined list. (You might pass it on the minister or church council.)

Now ask everyone to list three ways they would like the church to change in the future. It might be a new way of grouping, a different activity, more time spent on..., teaching about..., a chance to meet..., discuss this..., try that.... (If someone has well-known bees in their bonnet, this is not the moment to make endless speeches about them. Rather it is an opportunity to listen to each other, honestly, before God.)

Examine your proposals, word them well. Then pass them on for others to consider. (Check: Are you being loving, truthful, tactful and positively constructive? If you sense you are abrasively rubbing rough edges off other people, think about your own sharp corners. Remember Ephesians 4:29-32 before you proceed.)

'I've often prayed that God would change my circumstances until I discovered that he seems to prefer to start by changing me.'

God be in my heart

YOUR COMMENTS

Coping with anger

- Read Ephesians 4:25-32. Notice how many verses mention speaking in some form.
- Jesus was angry without sinning (Mark 3:5, John 2:16). Moses reflected God's righteous anger (Exodus 32:19). Compare these examples with the elder brother (Luke 15:28). Why was each one angry?
- Share your own experience of being angry. What can you do to help one another recognize personal pride or pique as a source of anger that needs to be repented of and confessed?
- How should Christians deal with and express righteous anger. For example, how should we react to injustice?

Seeing ourselves in others

When we listen to ourselves we become more aware of our own needs. Here are some imaginary people in real situations. How might a Christian friend pray for them?

- Jane is 42, single, a city business woman. Her heart is telling her, 'I'm dreading the long holiday at Christmas time.'
- Alison is shy, 27, and explains, 'I don't want to join a house group, I wouldn't fit in.'
- Mary, a pensioner, says, 'But we've always had the service at 11am. It was lovely when Canon Basil took it. They tried to change the time in the 50s but we knew it wouldn't work.'
- Karen sits down to heed her friend's tale of woe. But her inner voice is screaming, 'I'm tired of other people's troubles. Why can't someone listen to me?'
- Helen's husband died five years ago. She says, 'Peter was such a good man, why did God take him? I can't seem to get going without him. He was churchwarden and sang in the choir. He was always there when I needed him.'
- This autumn, Lucy's home seems empty. She finds it unsettling now Chris her youngest has left home for his training and the older two are married. She thinks, 'What's the matter with me? I ought to go out, volunteer for something, not moon around the house all day. I'm only 48!'

By myself

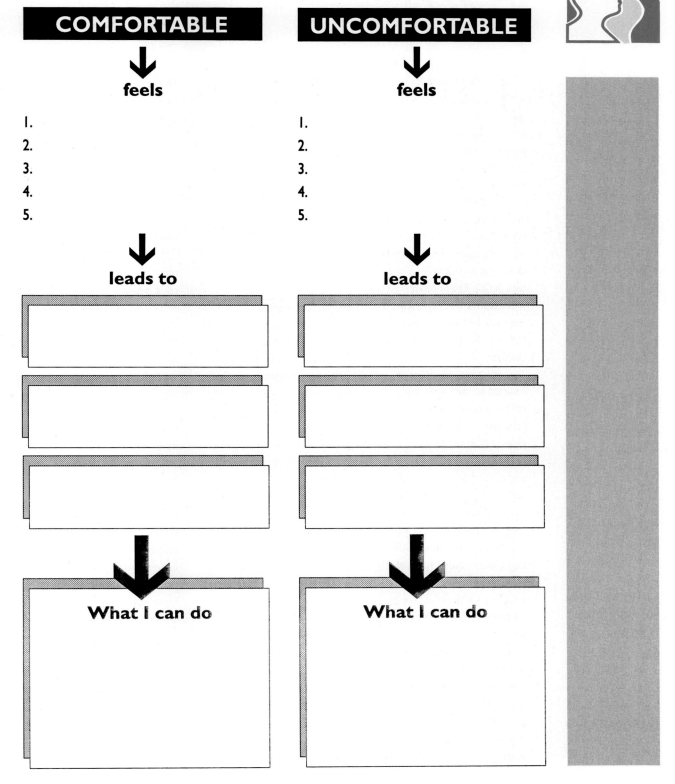

COMFORTABLE

⬇

feels

1.
2.
3.
4.
5.

⬇

leads to

UNCOMFORTABLE

⬇

feels

1.
2.
3.
4.
5.

⬇

leads to

⬇

What I can do

⬇

What I can do

Listening to Young People

I didn't find that mothering came naturally. My unfortunate daughter was subject to experiment and improvisation throughout her early years. I wanted to do so much for my baby and never knew exactly what her needs were. The relief of being able to communicate with her when she began to talk was wonderful. I have often wondered if that experience is responsible for the great need I have to talk to and listen to my children.

I started to pray with my children as soon as I was pregnant. I was aware, especially in my first pregnancy, of the baby responding to music, so it seemed reasonable that they would also respond to special conversation with God, in prayer. Later, in those endless night-time hours I spent trying to comfort my sleepless daughter (why did it take me 18 months to discover that leaving the light on worked wonders?), I talked to, sang to, and prayed with my baby. Not silently, but giving voice to all my fears and frustrations. On good days I was able to give thanks—and mean it. Did sharing all those words with my daughter start to shape the way that we can communicate now?

As they grow

The small child revels in 'talk'. They experiment with new words, try novel sentence structures and astound the hearer by repeating complex statements as though they understand them.

Establishing a good conversational habit with small children is important and very rewarding. As the child grows into some independence there are events to report, opinions to be aired, ideas to be shared. Parents and children bring their different experiences together and develop a shared understanding of the Christian way of life.

Praying together is part of the 'specialness'. Demonstrating how to construct prayers helps to establish a way of working that the child can make their own as they mature. Teaching our children to talk to God is a privilege.

Older children

Suddenly, overnight, the chatterbox falls silent. Enquiries about friends, school and outings are met with a grunt.

The bewildered parent steps back, rebuffed, and wonders when communication will be resumed. The child who demanded a cuddle yesterday closes the bedroom door today.

Our temptation to charge in and demand an explanation vies with the sadness that our child doesn't want us any more. But we are needed. Our child needs constancy in a world that is suddenly changing. Over-reacting — or seeming not to react at all—is not helpful. We need to continue to be honest about our feelings and wait for the child to discover that they are still accepted, loved and valued by the family.

Finding quality time for our children is essential. Not the half-ear we give as we watch the TV news, or the spotlight interrogation of the perpetrator of some wrong-doing, but a period when the child can know that they have our undivided attention. Our hands may be engaged in some mundane task but our ears, mind and heart belong exclusively to the sharer for as long as they need them. And *sharing* is usually what the older child is looking for.

I've always insisted that we have our main meal together, however inconvenient this might be. The meal is eaten round the table and the television is switched off. In early teen years this was viewed as a parental fixation. But my daughter, now 20, looks back and agrees that spending exclusive time together was a very important confirmation of an individual's importance within the family group.

This does not mean that guests are excluded from the meal table. Bringing in a different point of view is a very valuable way of helping teenagers to weigh opinion and examine their own understanding of a topic. But the expectation that the family will be available to listen, to express an opinion and to share their experience at a meal-time gives a sense of worth to the individual member, adult and child alike.

TV and talk
The television can be a wonderful tool for helping us to share difficult topics with our children! The dutiful parent may well turn off the television when an 'unsuitable' programme is expected. But the parent is not always going to be around to switch off the set, and many of the programmes that parents dislike are the ones that are going to be discussed at school the next day. Are we going to allow the ideas of uninformed classmates to be the ones taken on by our children? Or are we going to watch the programme with them so that we can share conversation about the topic, how it was presented, and what God's point of view might be?

It is most likely that the programme we find difficult treats sexuality as a tradable commodity or a cheap thrill. If our children are to develop a real understanding of God's will for human sexuality, they need to learn it from their parents. They also need to understand that the topic is a proper one for a family to discuss and that their parents are aware of the problems and pressures that a teenager faces.

Towards independence
I do think it important that parents, especially mothers, do not allow themselves to become servants. It is the responsibility of parents to encourage their children to become useful, independent adults. That means household tasks are shared, everyone learns how to operate the washing machine, cook nutritious meals, clean the bathroom and do the ironing.

We should be expecting our child to take on increasing responsibility for their own lives. But that can mean having to watch them be late for school yet again. Handing over a clothing allowance allows our young adult to make money decisions. But it also means that we will have to see money being spent unwisely. Letting them go to bed in their own time may mean black rings around the eyes in the morning. Allowing them to

Saying sorry
When a child does wrong we expect confession and a request for forgiveness. When parents wrong a child it is vital that they, too, admit their guilt and ask forgiveness of the child.

God our Father
- God made us—individually, specifically, intentionally. There are no 'spares'.
- God loves us—unconditionally.
- God doesn't remember past, forgiven mistakes.
- God never gives up on us.
- God treats us as thinking people, even when our behaviour indicates that we are not!
- God is never too busy to listen.
- God always meets us more than half way.
- God doesn't gossip or tell tales.
- God inspires, instructs; he never forces.
- God has set us the example of 'how to' in Jesus—he puts theory into practice.
- God never says 'that's enough, I can't take any more'.
- God always lets us try again.

'Listening is not thinking about what we are going to say when the other person has stopped talking.'

Norman H Wright

decide which church service to go to may mean they don't attend church at all.

All this is essential, however, if we are to sleep soundly when our young person leaves home and lives completely free of our influence. If we don't allow our children space to get things wrong, we don't allow them the opportunity to get things right! If there's no room for trying things out, the young person has no experience of how to cope with adult situations. If there has been no discussion about difficult topics, the newly independent young adult may find himself or herself cast adrift. They have relied on a parent to do all the thinking for them.

So often it seems that the aspects we like least about our children are the ones we like least about ourselves. And the problems we fret about over our children are frequently the ones that tried our parents most! Can we honestly say we were never out too late, always got our homework in on time or didn't go out with an unsuitable partner?

Remembering ourselves as developing adults can be very helpful in learning how to listen to and support our maturing children.

Being there
Sometimes it seems impossible to hear or understand what a child is saying. We are trying to listen, to be a supportive parent, but our offspring is not communicating.

The frustration of wanting, but not being allowed, to help can hurt. But sometimes all we can do as parents is to be there. Not there as an hotel or free dinner, but there as a consistent, reliable home base. Our no means no, but our yes means certainly.

The transition from dependent child to independent adult can be a difficult time. The parent has to learn to let go, and the child has to learn to make proper use of his or her liberation.

A perfect model
The way in which God cares for us, his children, is a perfect model for the way in which we should be caring for our children as they grow towards independence. We should take comfort in the fact that although God's care for us is perfect, the way that we develop and behave most certainly is not! That is because we have free will and do not always choose God's way.

Our children have free will too, and we have to understand that they will not always accept our will for them. Sometimes they will be influenced by friends and want to follow the crowd. Sometimes they will be 'out of sorts' and not want to do anything that might appear to be co-operating! Sometimes we will have to accept that we are not all-wise and totally informed, and we may not have suggested the best course of action. Parents can get it wrong too.

Try, try again
How does God treat us? Does he force us to do what is right? Does he lecture us about repeating the same, stupid, avoidable sins? No, he waits until we show the smallest sign of wanting to leave our unwise path and comes to meet us joyfully. Jesus' parable about the prodigal son is really about the welcoming and forgiving father.

He forgives us. But then comes the hardest part: God allows us freedom to choose again and perhaps this time demonstrate that we can live as responsible, loving adults.

If we try to love our children as God loves us we will certainly be listening, supportive parents. And we will remember that God always allows us the opportunity to try again.

Founded on love

A family is founded on love. Every family originates from the love, however imperfect, of one human being for another. Yet too often we lose sight of the standard to which we aspired at the start of our relationship. We need to remind ourselves of the ideal to be worked towards, so that we don't become bogged down in every-day muddle.

Sincerity

The apostle Paul talks about human relationships in Romans, chapter 12. 'Love must be sincere', he writes in verse 9. The word used for sincere means 'without wax'. Sculptors whose work was less than perfect were known to use wax to patch up the defects and make them invisible to the casual viewer. Close inspection would reveal just how much covering up had been going on and, of course, exposure to heat would melt the wax and leave the work looking very sad! How can family love be 'without wax'?

Honour

'Honour one another', says verse 10. Why is it that we 'always hurt the one we love' to quote an old song? We sometimes say things to members of our family that we'd be ashamed to have overheard by outsiders! Why do we find it much easier to honour our next-door neighbour than our next of kin?

Sharing

'Share with God's people who are in need' is the challenge of verse 13. It's easy to appreciate the needs of someone who's got a broken leg or who's just had a baby. How might our teenagers be 'God's people in need'?

Harmony

'Live in harmony with one another,' Paul says in verse 16. My dictionary defines harmony as 'agreement, concord, peace' and 'melodious sound'. Creating a melodious sound in an orchestra takes planning and practice. Do we allow ourselves enough time for rehearsal, or do we expect to be able to sight-read our way through family life? Or consider the way that unions negotiate with management, nation with nation, to reach agreement, concord, peace. Are these helpful models for a way to greater family harmony?

Humility

'Do not be proud, but be willing to associate with people of low position. Do not be conceited' (verse 16). Parents are right to encourage their children, to commend their efforts. But parents need to beware of pushing their children to fulfil their own, parental ambitions. It is difficult, too, for some parents to accept that they have been given a normal, healthy, average child! Are we able to accept our children as the people God has made them to be? Or are we quietly trying to improve on his work?

Justice

'Be careful to do what is right in the eyes of everybody', verse 17. Family justice is not always easy to appreciate, especially if you are the member whose rights seem to have been violated. 'It's not fair, they're always the favourite!' How can we be more careful?

Good over evil

'Do not be overcome by evil, but overcome evil with good,' verse 21. It is possible to feel that there's no hope, things will never get better. What 'good' can we employ to overcome the aspects of family life that we find hardest to cope with?

'Love must be sincere. Hate what is evil; cling to what is good. Be devoted to one another in brotherly love. Honour one another above yourselves.'

Romans 12:9-10

GROUP IDEAS

Young ones

Divide group into 4s and 5s. Have ready glue, quantities of colour magazines, scissors and a large sheet of paper for each group. Ask the participants to produce a montage about how they remember themselves as teenagers: the things they liked, did, bought, enjoyed etc. Fashions change but teenagers are teenagers!

Allow about 20 minutes. Participants can then go around the room and talk to others interpreting the montages. Or the montages can be shared in turn with the whole group, allowing for comments, questions, fun and laughter.

GROUP IDEAS

Two-way communication

Select two volunteers (A and B). Give A a simple outline of, say, a building such as a church or a castle. This must not be shown to B who is told to follow the instructions given by A and to redraw the picture. No questions are allowed. Allow 3 minutes.

Before B's effort is shown to everyone, repeat the procedure with a third volunteer, C. However, C can ask questions and seek clarification.

Compare the two pictures and discuss the difficulties of communication. Talk about the feelings experienced by A, B, and C. (This exercise could be done with the whole group as B and C.)

GROUP IDEAS

Ups and downs

Make a board game in the style of Ludo or Snakes & Ladders , but in the shape of a house. Divide the house into numbered squares (not more than 40). Label some squares with a large question mark. Photocopy the board on to A4 sheets for each group. The aim of the game is to move through all the squares according to the shake of dice and the contents of penalty/reward cards called *family cards*.

The *family cards* relate to a typical family: mother (the player), Bill (husband), Sue and Tom (children). The cards either describe positive reactions (such as, 'showed genuine interest in Sue's latest CD') or negative reactions (such as 'no time to listen to Tom's football saga today'). Make 10 cards of each type and indicate the number of squares to move backwards or forwards. Then mix among them six cards which record reactions which some would regard as positive, others negative (such as, 'I told Sue she is old enough to please herself whether or not she goes to church'). On these cards don't indicate the squares to move.

When a player falls on a **?** square she must pick up a *family card* and move forwards or backwards as indicated. Replace cards at the bottom of the pile. If the card doesn't indicate the number of squares to move, ask the group to decide whether the player should move forwards or backwards, and by how much. Don't replace these cards.

When a player reaches the last square, stop the game and discuss the emotions and situations the group has passed through. Were the rewards or penalties on the *family cards* appropriate?

Never in my family!

Family problems come in all shapes and sizes. Usually we react instinctively because we haven't had time to think things through. The following list is entirely fictitious, but every family has to cope with these kind of problems.

Give time to think about coping with these situations. How might we respond? How should we respond?

- Peter is 15 and has stated that he doesn't believe in God, so he's not going to go to church. The vicar wants to talk to him.
- Katy has started on an art course. The older people at church are openly critical of her new hairstyle and the rings in her ears and nose.
- The school has telephoned to ask if you are aware that your 17-year-old son has been skipping lessons.
- The vicar's daughter has just come home from her second year at university, pregnant.
- Mike is becoming increasingly withdrawn. He left school with reasonable exam results and good references but he can't get a job.
- Sara is in love. Exams are looming, but she can't think past the next time she'll see her boyfriend.
- Richard is refusing to see Aunty because he says she's too old. And anyway he saw her last month.
- The boys' room is a pigsty and it's driving you to distraction.
- Anne wants to paint her room herself, and she wants to paint it black.
- Your neighbour has just seen your 16-year-old son come out of the supermarket with a multi-pack of canned beer.
- Carolyn can never make up her mind: should she go to the local college and live at home, or move away to a better course?
- Tim has decided to go vegetarian in a household of meat eaters.
- The empty packet in her bin suggests that Elizabeth is on the pill.
- Your son seems to buying more goods than he should have the money for. Could it be the explanation for the money that disappears from your purse?

Listening to Group Members

Over the years women's groups have played an important part in the life and witness of the local church. They have been:

- effective in out-reach
- unthreatening gatherings to which it has been easy to invite a neighbour or a friend
- a bridge into membership of the church
- an opportunity for teaching the faith
- faithful in caring for people
- willing to accept tasks which need doing—flower arranging, cleaning, serving cups of tea and coffee.

All change

Changes in society are affecting women's groups. More and more women go out to work and not just young mothers. Women, once the family is off their hands, look for a job. Their skills, resourcefulness and reliability are valued.

As we move towards the end of the century, economists predict that there will be as many women as men who 'go out to work'. They may accept more part-time jobs than men, but the belief that women should stay at home is dying, if it has not died already.

The task of a leader is to listen—to listen to the needs of those who come to the group and, just as importantly, to listen to the needs of women in the church and community. It's so easy to settle into the traditional way of running a group without considering how the group should change to accommodate the needs of those who *don't yet* come.

Facing Change

Few of us like to face change. It makes us feel unsettled and insecure. We don't like moving into unfamiliar territory. Yet being a Christian is really all about being changed. 'If anyone is in Christ, he is a new creation, the old has gone the new has come.' (2 Corinthians 5:17.) And the Bible tells us we 'are being transformed (changed) into Christ's likeness with ever-increasing glory which comes from the Lord who is the Spirit.' (2 Corinthians 3:18.) When our faith and security is in God we can face change and adjust accordingly and grow. It may be right to recognize that the ministry among women in our churches needs to change.

Introducing change

If your group is to change, the way you introduce this is very important.

- Help the group feel to involved.
- Help them to understand why changes are being made.
- Invite them to pray about it all.
- Ask for their thoughts and ideas.
- Help them to see the need of being the kind of group to which new members can feel welcome.

Hard questions

Let's ask some questions:

- Is the meeting the 'hymn sandwich' it has been for years?
- Are you singing out of a very old hymnbook?
- Do the women sit passively listening (or nodding off) while everything is controlled from the front?
- Is it the same week in, week out, year in, year out?

Such meetings have been a blessing. I have led and spoken at this kind of meeting and been aware of a sense of fellowship and warmth. However, I'm not so sure they are appealing to today's woman.

How do we change?

Are there things we can do to make the *place* more user-friendly?

Learning to Listen © CPAS 1993

Arrange to go into the meeting room with two or three of your helpers. Together look at what might be done. Ideas will flow. We live in warm, comfortable and attractive homes yet invite people to come into a bare and very worn church hall.

I am very aware that money is often the problem, as well as the fact the hall is used by different organizations and age groups. But don't let this stop us from taking a long, hard look, and using our imagination.

Consider:
- Some colourful banners and posters.
- Chairs in a half circle rather than in straight rows.
- A rug or two to add warmth (but be careful they can't be tripped over).
- Some colourful cushions on the chairs.

Think through *when* you meet. Would a morning meeting starting with coffee be more acceptable than, say, Thursday at 3pm? After lunch it can be hard for people to keep their eyes open as they get older.

Would women like to call in on their way from shopping? From time to time a light lunch could be laid on.

Are women with work commitments able to make the times you meet? Do the meetings end in time to allow mothers to pick up young children from school? You may find a bit of informal 'market research' helpful. Ask people in your church what changes would be most suitable for them.

Encourage *participation*. Give women the freedom to chip in with a comment—or share a personal experience. The leader needs to be able to handle such interruptions with sensitivity and love. Watch out for those who always have something to say! A sense of humour will help. Laughter is a tonic and a sign that members are enjoying themselves. Encourage it.

Review the *programme*. You need to do this from time to time as the group changes and different needs come to the surface. Are there more interesting ways of using the

hour together? Are the subjects relevant to the women you want to attract?

Keep the *welcome*. More important than where you meet or how you arrange the programme is the warmth of welcome which women receive. Let women feel that they are wanted—not just to add to the numbers, but because they matter and the meeting has something to offer them.

'Love is not so much a matter of being willing to listen as of wanting to hear.'

Alan Glendining

Do's and Don'ts

Remember:
- Don't show favouritism.
- Don't make a person feel guilty if they have to miss a meeting.
- Don't fuss and try to carry everyone's burdens.

and
- It's sometimes right to say 'no' when you are asked to do something.
- Pray, pray, for God cares and is at work.
- Love is the way: love for God and others.

What me a leader?

You may have been the leader of a women's group for many years. Perhaps you are running out of ideas; you're in a bit of a rut. Or maybe you have just been asked to take on a group. You're feeling nervous and inexperienced. What does the group, and what does God, require in a 'leader'?

A leader is required to be someone who:

♦ Has a real relationship with God through Jesus Christ.
♦ Is a faithful member of the church, known and respected by the group.
♦ Is open to God and, through prayer and obedience, is sensitive to how he is leading.
♦ Loves and cares about people.
♦ Is non-threatening and approachable.
♦ Knows how to listen, keeps confidences and never gossips.

Don't feel discouraged because you feel you're not an ideal leader. You're in good company. Remember Moses when the Lord called him? His reply was, 'Who am I that I should go?' He was full of questions and doubts about himself. And the Lord's reply was, 'I will be with you.' You may say, 'But I'm not Moses.' But God is still God. When God called Jeremiah he said, 'I do not know how to

speak.' (Know the feeling?) And the Lord's reply was, 'Do not be afraid... I am with you.'

We're tempted to look for a good leader. The Lord looks for a believer who he equips and gifts for the task.

Length of leadership

How long should a leader stay on? Some people in a church hold back from taking on positions of leadership because they fear they will have the task forever. And there are leaders who have been in the job for years and really do need to pull out. 'But there is no one willing to take over,' is the usual response. It might be true. The danger is we're looking for a perfect leader with all the right qualities and gifts. God isn't.

So, how long? Three to five years is a good period.

Shared leadership

Why do we always think in terms of one person being in charge? Sharing the leadership is valuable. It can be a lonely task, and to have one or more with whom a leader can share and pray will make such a difference.

If you are building up a small team to share the work and develop gifts, aim to meet

regularly, say once a month. These can be prayer and planning meetings when you can :

♦ Pray together.
♦ Share how you feel about how things are going.
♦ Look at the needs of the group or individuals.
♦ Plan future programmes and events.

Vision

Look out as a leader for training days when your own vision can be enlarged and new ideas learnt. Ministry Among Women (which is part of CPAS) runs workshops in different parts of the country. If there are no meetings in your area, contact CPAS to see if they can help.

Going into action

Each leader will have her own style of leading a meeting. This she will develop as she grows in confidence.

However, guard against seeing your identity, worth and status in your role as leader rather than as a Christian and part of the body of Christ. It is possible to become very possessive of your little patch.

Pastoral care

Possibly the most important side to the ministry among women is the care we give to each member. But leaders should never feel they have to solve every problem that comes their way. Leaders are there to draw alongside someone in need, caring and listening.

Dr Marion Ashton, a well-known counsellor and speaker, says that belonging to God and his family can bring:
Significance—as a child of infinite worth to God.

Acceptance—loved and forgiven by God.
Achievement—needed by God for service in his Kingdom.

Many people want someone to listen, rather than to solve their problems. They need space to think it through and decide for themselves. A good listener creates that space rather than dictates solutions. In all our listening it is vital to keep confidences. There must not even be 'a sharing of a confidence for prayer'. Sharing

can easily turn into gossip.

Out of your depth
From time to time you will be faced with another's problem in which you feel out of your depth. Recognize your own limits of skills, emotions and time. Be honest and suggest that the person seeks further help from a doctor, minister or local Christian counselling service. Your minister should have telephone numbers of the support services in your area.

> 'The Christian is called out of insignificance into significance.'
>
> **William Barclay**

Areas of pastoral care

Bereavement The loss of a husband sometimes leads a woman to join a group. A widow will appreciate being able to talk about her husband without people trying to change the subject. And she'll welcome an invitation into another's home or to join an outing.

Low self image A woman's status and identity can be in the fact that she is someone's wife or mother. She has yet to learn to accept that she is a person in her own right. She needs to come to a greater awareness of God's love for her. And she will experience this acceptance as she is loved and made to feel of value by others. The group's love will demonstrate and make believable the Bible's astounding claim that God loves us as we are.

Depression Most people can get down in the dumps at times but real depression needs medical help. Again the support of a praying and loving fellowship can do wonders although great patience is needed.

Loneliness A high percentage of people live alone. When a family grows up a mother can feel she is no longer needed. She has lost her role in life. The single person, too, who has cared for elderly parents, can feel very lonely when they die.

Sick and housebound Housebound people are easily forgotten. A visit will be valued. But why not encourage others in the group to keep in touch, too? Some churches tape their services and these can be distributed. Keep in touch with your minister as the housebound person may want to receive Holy Communion at home.

Unconverted husband Great sensitivity is required to consider the feelings of a non-Christian partner. A husband can feel that the church is taking over— and taking his place in—his wife's life. The wife can try too hard to bring her husband to Christ. Someone has said it is wiser to talk much to God about a husband, and rather less to the husband about God.

GROUP IDEAS

Senior appointment

The job of leading the women's group in your church (of which you are a member) is to be advertised. Ask your group to write the advertisement for the church magazine or local newspaper.

You may want to divide the group into smaller sub-groups. Ask them to write the job description of the leader of your group detailing hours of work, contract, tasks to be done, skills needed, experience necessary, personal qualities, etc.

Collate the findings, using an OHP or a flip chart. Discuss, and then pray for all in leadership roles in the church.

GROUP IDEAS

Discovering gifts

Read through 1 Corinthians 12. Mention some of the gifts which you see in members of your group. Don't embarrass—do encourage.

GROUP IDEAS

Brainstorm

Using OHP or flip chart, write up suggestions from the entire group on the kind of subjects they would like included in any future programme. Only if absolutely necessary ask for clarification.

In groups of 3 - 6 plan a series of six meetings on a specific theme, which the groups choose for themselves. Ask them to suggest ideas for a variety of presentation.

GROUP IDEAS

Areas to explore

1. What is the place and purpose of the women's group in your church?

2. In what ways does it need to adapt to today's circumstances?

3. How can we help new members to feel they really belong? If a new person hasn't joined your group during the past year, why might this be?

4. What will someone gain from the woman's group that they may not find anywhere else?

GROUP IDEAS

No way in

Ask a group to stand in a circle, talking to each other. Another woman comes in and tries to join the circle—she walks round and round and finds no way in, no welcome.

Then let her walk round again, but ask the circle to open up and receive her into it—not in an overwhelming way but naturally.

Let one or two others try this. Talk together afterwards about how it felt. What can we learn from these experiences?

Learning to Listen © CPAS 1993

On to the next century

Life for women in the late twentieth century is different! In every preceding period women have been reasonably sure about their position in society and the roles they have to play. Previously, women were largely aware of what was expected of them and usually accepted their own roles of home maker and carer of children, with perhaps an occasional grumble.

Today, however, it's all change. The new thinking is launched from every hoarding; it is found in most television advertisements and it is slipped, seemingly innocuously, between the pages of women's magazines. We may well laugh at some of the adverts but, if we are honest, we will still find ourselves struggling to become the sort of women they show. Somehow, we have been made to feel failures and old fashioned if we do not conform to these 'modern' ideas.

What, then, are some of the ideas about women which the advertisers would like us to believe? List ideas from TV, magazines, newspapers, radio etc. Build up a portrait or even caricature of the 'modern woman'. What are her fashions, style, leisure pursuits, family life, work and so on?

Think of a previous era, say the 20s and 30s or post war 40s - 60s. Make a list of the kind of life and expectations of women then. Listen to someone who was working and raising a family in one of those periods. Now have fun as you compare these two lists.

♦ What have we got now that is better for us? What are we sorry has been lost and gone forever?
♦ Does the Bible help us to see how we can live in a contemporary, changing world? (Proverbs 3:5-26, Matthew 6:19-7:12, Philippians 1:27-2:15, Hebrews 12:1-3).
♦ Can we help those who have lived in previous generations to understand the present generation?
♦ Have we the right attitude to those who are living in the modern world but know nothing of what it was like to be brought up in pre-war Britain or even during the war years and after?
♦ How should our group and its programme change and adapt to be relevant today?

BOOKLIST

CPAS code	Title	Author and Publisher
03429	**A Mind at Ease**	Marion Ashton, Overcomer
05321	**Temptations Women Face**	Mary Ellen Ashcroft, Kingsway
92023	**Women Alone?**	Kathy Keay, Bible Society
92024	**Women in the Church**	Rhoda Hiscox, Bible Society
92025	**Women in the World**	Jeni Parsons, Bible Society
92026	**Women at Home**	Kathy Keay, Bible Society
92010	**Learning from Four Women**	Joyce Jelbart & Rachel Harden, CPAS

These resources are available from CPAS Sales by quoting the 1993 code number.

Other Relevant Resources

Listening	Anne Long, Darton Longman & Todd
The Wisdom to Listen	Michael Mitton, Grove Booklets
Listening to God	Joyce Huggett, Hodder & Stoughton
Listen and Live	Colin Urquhart, Hodder & Stoughton
My Dear Child	Colin Urquhart, Hodder & Stoughton
My Dear Son	Colin Urquhart, Hodder & Stoughton
Open to God	Joyce Huggett, Hodder & Stoughton
Listening to Others	Joyce Huggett, Hodder & Stoughton
Friend in Need	Selwyn Hughes, Kingsway
How to Give Away Your Faith	Paul Little, IVP
Space for God	David Runcom, Hodder & Stoughton
Emotions: Can You Trust Them?	James Dobson, Hodder & Stoughton
Dare to Discipline	James Dobson, Kingsway
Understanding Teenagers	Steve Chalke, Kingsway Pocketbooks
Teens Speak Out	Josh McDowell, Scripture Press
Understanding Adolescence	Roger Hurding, Hodder & Stoughton
So You've Got Teenage Children	John & Janet Houghton, Kingsway

CPAS, Athena Drive, Tachbrook Park, WARWICK CV34 6NG.
Telephone: (0926) 334242. Orderline: (0926) 335855.